THE FABULOUS LOST & FOUND

AND THE LITTLE ALBANIAN MOUSE

WRITTEN BY MARK PALLIS
ILLUSTRATED BY PETER BAYNTON

NEU WESTEND
— PRESS —

Etrita - thanks! - MP

For Hannah and Skye - PB

THE FABULOUS LOST & FOUND AND THE LITTLE ALBANIAN MOUSE
Copyright text © 2020 Mark Pallis and Copyright images © 2020 Peter Baynton

All rights reserved. This book or any portion thereof may not be reproduced or used in any manner whatsoever without the express written permission of the publisher except for the use of brief excerpts in a review.

First Printing, 2020
ISBN: 978-1-913595-21-0
NeuWestendPress.com

THE FABULOUS LOST & FOUND

AND THE LITTLE ALBANIAN MOUSE

WRITTEN BY MARK PALLIS
ILLUSTRATED BY PETER BAYNTON

NEU WESTEND
— PRESS —

In the middle of the big city is a tiny yellow building. If anyone loses anything, this is where it ends up.

It is called the Lost and Found.

Mr and Mrs Frog keep everything safe, hoping that someday every lost watch and bag and phone and toy and shoe and cheesegrater will find its owner again.

But the shop is very small. And there are so many lost things. It is all quite a squeeze, but still, it's fabulous.

One sunny day, a little mouse walked in.

"Welcome," said Mrs Frog. "What have you lost?"

"Kam humbur kapelen," said the mouse.

Mr and Mrs Frog could not speak Albanian. They had no idea what the little mouse was saying.

What shall we do? they wondered.

Maybe she's lost an umbrella. Everyone loses an umbrella at least twice, thought Mr Frog.

"Have you lost this?" asked Mr Frog.

"Një ombrellë? Jo," replied the mouse.

Then Mrs Frog remembered something that had been handed in a few months ago...

"Is this yours?" Mrs Frog asked, holding up a chunk of cheese.

"Djathë? Jo. Vjen erë e keqe!" said the mouse.

"Time to put that cheese in the bin dear," said Mr Frog.

"Maybe the word 'kapelë' means coat," said Mr Frog.

"Now where did I put that nice yellow one?"

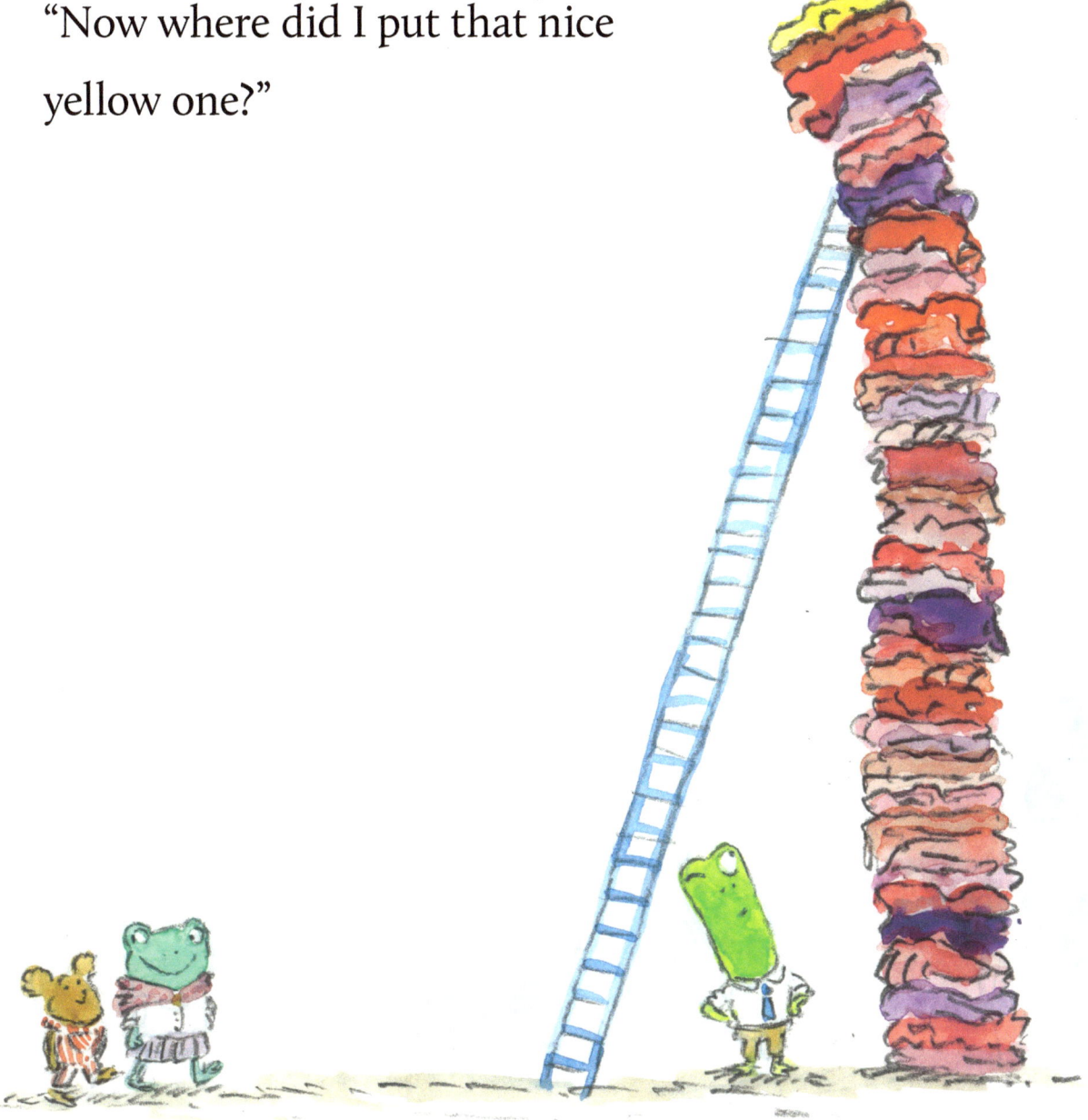

"Got it!" said Mr Frog.

"Një pallto? Jo. Kam humbur kapelen," said the mouse.

She was starting to feel a bit frustrated.

"We need to keep trying," said Mrs Frog.

Jo shallin.

Jo pantallonat.

Jo trikon.

Jo syzet e diellit.

Jo këpucët.

"Kam humbur kapelen," said the mouse.

Jo tre libra.

Jo katër banane.

Jo pesë çelësa.

It was no good. A fat wet tear rolled down the mouse's cheek.

"How about a nice cup of tea?" asked Mrs Frog kindly.

"Më pëlqen shumë çaji. Faleminderit," replied the mouse.
They sat together, sipping their tea and all feeling a bit sad.

Suddenly, the mouse realised she could try pointing.

She pointed at her head.
"Kapelë!" she said.

"I've got it!" exclaimed Mrs Frog, leaping up.

"A wig of course!" said Mrs Frog.

"Jo një parukë," said the mouse.

Jo një parukë e kuqe.

Jo bjonde.

Jo kafe.

Jo e shumëngjyrëshme.

Jo jeshile.

"What about this?" asked Mr Frog, pulling back a curtain.

"Kapelë!" exclaimed the mouse.

"Ah, so 'kapelë' means hat. Wonderful," smiled Mr and Mrs Frog.

Shumë e vogël.

Shumë e madhe.

Shumë e gjatë.

Shumë e ngushtë.

"One hat left," said Mrs Frog, reaching all the way to the back of the cupboard.

"It couldn't be this old thing, could it?"

"Kapelja ime.

Kam gjetur kapelen time!

Faleminderit shumë," said the mouse.

And just like that, the mouse found her hat.

"Mirupafshim," she said, as she skipped away.
"Mirupafshim," replied Mr and Mrs Frog.

"I wonder who will come tomorrow?" said Mr Frog.
Mrs Frog put her arm around him.

"I don't know," she replied, giving him a squeeze,
"but whoever it is, we'll do our best to help."

LEARNING TO LOVE LANGUAGES

An additional language opens a child's mind, broadens their horizons and enriches their emotional life. Research has shown that the time between a child's birth and their sixth or seventh birthday is a "golden period" when they are most receptive to new languages. This is because they have an in-built ability to distinguish the sounds they hear and make sense of them. The Story-powered Language Learning Method taps into these natural abilities.

HOW THE STORY-POWERED LANGUAGE LEARNING METHOD WORKS

We create an emotionally engaging and funny story for children and adults to enjoy together, just like any other picture book. Studies show that social interaction, like enjoying a book together, is critical in language learning.

Through the story, we introduce a relatable character who speaks only in the new language. This helps build empathy and a positive attitude towards people who speak different languages. These are both important aspects in laying the foundations for lasting language acquisition in a child's life.

As the story progresses, the child naturally works with the characters to discover the meanings of a wide range of fun new words. Strategic use of humour ensures that this subconscious learning is rewarded with laughter; the child feels good and the first seeds of a lifelong love of languages are sown.

For more information and free downloads visit www.neuwestendpress.com

ALL THE BEAUTIFUL ALBANIAN WORDS AND PHRASES FROM OUR STORY

kam humbur kapelen	I've lost my hat
ombrellë	umbrella
djathë	cheese
vjen erë e keqe	stinks
pallto	coat
shall	scarf
pantallonat	trousers
syzet e diellit	sunglasses
triko	sweater
këpucët	shoes
një	one
dy	two
tre	three
katër	four
pesë	five
kompjuter	computer
libër	book
çelës	key
biçikletë	bicycle
banane	banana
më pëlqen shumë çaji	I love tea
faleminderit	thanks
parukë	wig
E kuqe (f) i kuq (m)	red
bjonde	blond
kafe	brown
jeshile (f) jeshil (m)	green
shumëngjyrësh	multicoloured
jo	no
kapelja ime	my hat
shumë e gjatë (f) shumë i gjatë (m)	too tall
Shumë e madhe (f) Shumë i madh (m)	too big
shumë e vogël (f) shumë i vogël (m)	too small
shumë e ngushtë (f) shumë i ngushtë (m)	too tight
kam gjetur kapelen time	I've found my hat
faleminderit shumë	thank you very much
mirupafshim	goodbye

THE WORLD OF
THE FABULOUS LOST & FOUND

THIS STORY IS ALSO AVAILABLE IN...

FRENCH SPANISH

ITALIAN CZECH

KOREAN WELSH

GERMAN HEBREW

SWEDISH GREEK SLOVAKIAN

VIETNAMESE LATIN PORTUGUESE

...AND MANY MORE LANGUAGES!

@MARK_PALLIS ON TWITTER
WWW.MARKPALLIS.COM

ENJOYED IT?
WRITE A REVIEW AND
LET US KNOW!

@PETERBAYNTON ON INSTAGRAM
WWW.PETERBAYNTON.COM

www.ingramcontent.com/pod-product-compliance
Lightning Source LLC
Chambersburg PA
CBHW050757110526
44588CB00002B/32